Speedboats

Kate Riggs

CREATIVE EDUCATION • CREATIVE PAPERBACKS

seedlings

Published by Creative Education and Creative Paperbacks
P.O. Box 227, Mankato, Minnesota 56002
Creative Education and Creative Paperbacks are
imprints of The Creative Company
www.thecreativecompany.us

Design by Ellen Huber
Production by Chelsey Luther
Printed in the United States of America

Photographs by Alamy (DIOMEDIA, David Pick), Corbis
(Alan Schein Photography, Imaginechina), Getty Images
(Andy Newman/Florida Keys News Bureau), Newscom (Steve
Sparrow Cultura), Shutterstock (Darren Brode, fckncg, RUI
FERREIRA, Iakov Filimonov, Angelo Giampiccolo, holbox,
javarman, marijaf, megainarmy, Pedro Monteiro, Nerthuz,
Plutonius 3d, ruslylove, s_oleg, Jan S.), SuperStock (Buzz
Pictures)

Library of Congress Cataloging-in-Publication Data
Riggs, Kate.
Speedboats / Kate Riggs.
p. cm. — (Seedlings)
Summary: A kindergarten-level introduction to speedboats,
covering their speed, drivers, role in transportation, and
such defining features as their v-shape.
Includes index.
ISBN 978-1-60818-523-8 (hardcover)
ISBN 978-1-62832-123-4 (pbk)
1. Motorboats—Juvenile literature. I. Title. II. Series:
Seedlings.

GV835.R54 2015
387.2'31—dc23   2014000185

CCSS: RI.K.1, 2, 3, 4, 5, 6, 7;
RI.1.1, 2, 3, 4, 5, 6, 7; RF.K.1, 3; RF.1.1

First Edition
9 8 7 6 5 4 3 2 1

TABLE OF CONTENTS

Time to splash!

Speedboats are super fast boats. They race on rivers, lakes, and oceans.

Some speedboats have closed tops.

Other speedboats
have open tops.

Most speedboats are pointed in front.

Speedboats that look like airplanes are called hydroplanes.

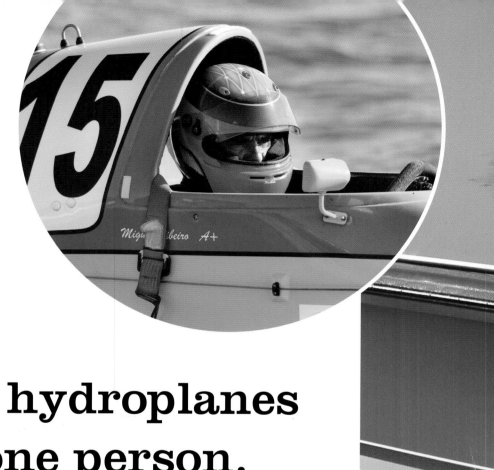

Small hydroplanes
hold one person.
Four or five people
can ride in bigger
go-fast boats.

Big go-fast boats have two or more engines.

Boats with more engines can go faster than boats with one engine.

A speedboat
bounces through
the water.

Water sprays and splashes behind it.

Go, speedboat,

go!

Picture a Speedboat

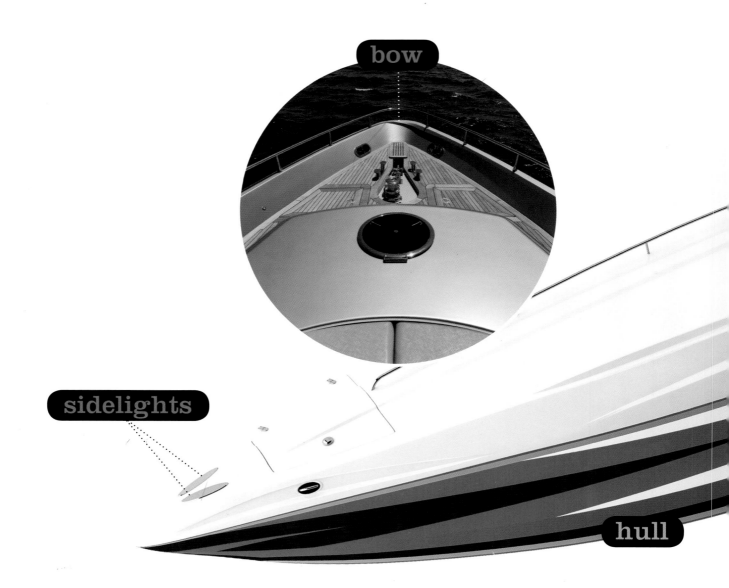

bow

sidelights

hull

gunwales

stern

engines

propeller

21

Words to Know

engines: machines inside vehicles that make them move

go-fast boats: speedboats with very pointy noses

hydroplanes: light, fast speedboats with parts called sponsons that stick out from the sides

oceans: big areas of deep, salty water

Read More

Von Finn, Denny. *Hydroplanes.*
Minneapolis: Bellwether Media, 2008.

Von Finn, Denny. *Powerboats.*
Minneapolis: Bellwether Media, 2010.

Websites

American Power Boat Association Videos
http://www.apba.org/video
Watch videos of speedboats in action!

Motorboat Coloring Page
http://www.hellokids.com/c_16790/coloring-pages
/transportation-coloring-pages/boat-coloring-pages/motor-boat
Print out this picture of a motorboat to color.

Index

WHAT'S INSIDE?

Photographs by Anthea Sieveking

Dial Books for Young Readers · New York

What's inside the drawer?

sweat shirt

undershirt

socks

sweat pants

underpants

What's inside the toy box?

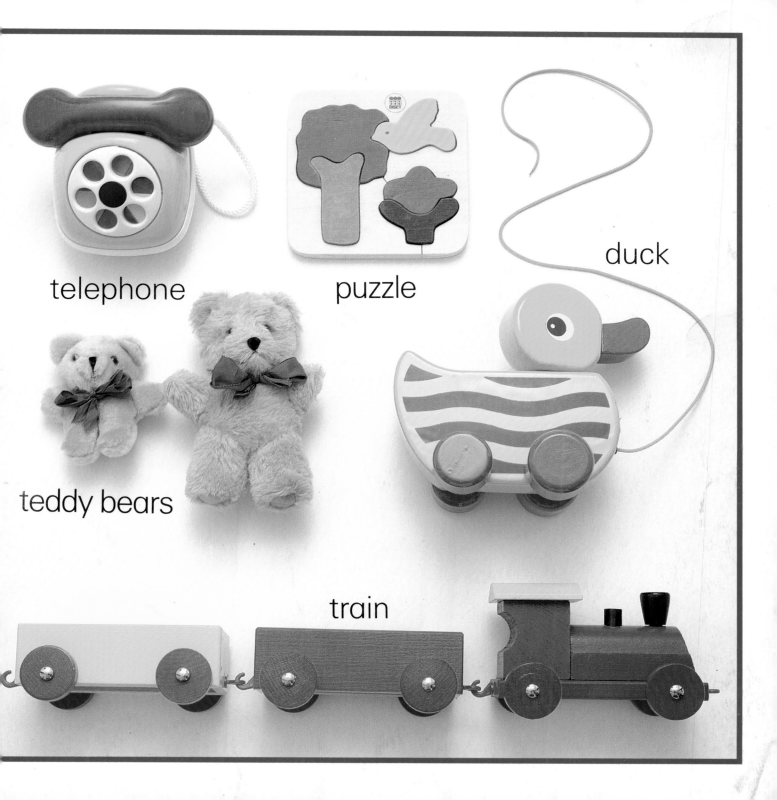

telephone

puzzle

duck

teddy bears

train

What's inside the changing bag?

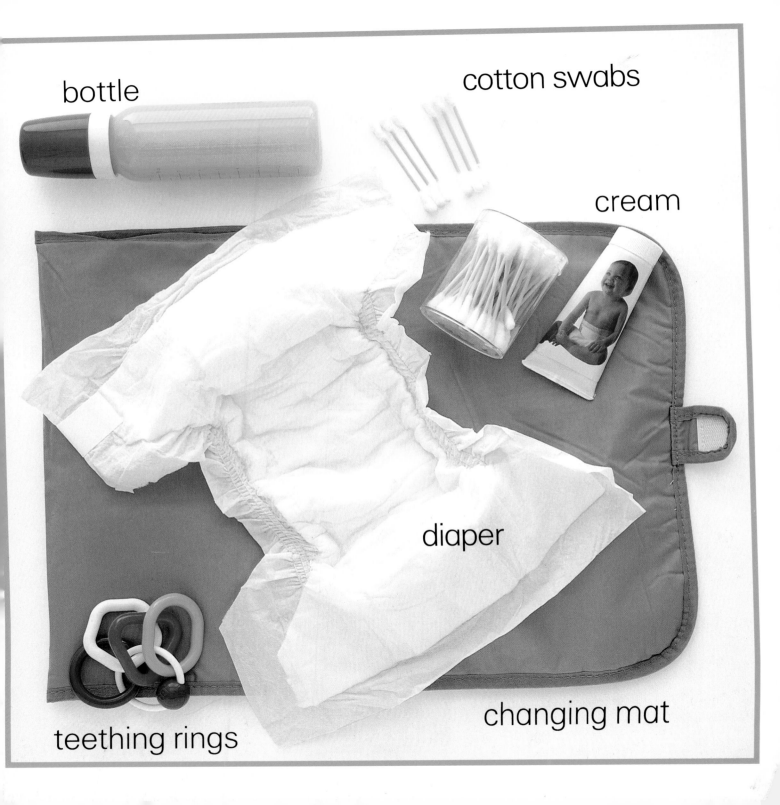

bottle

cotton swabs

cream

diaper

changing mat

teething rings

What's inside the kitchen cupboard?

wooden spoon

bowl

strainer

measuring
spoons

cookie cutter

saucepan

rolling pin

What's inside the shopping bags?

orange

grapes

apple

pear

banana

What's inside
the picnic basket?

spoon

cup

fork

knife

plate

What's inside the beach bag?

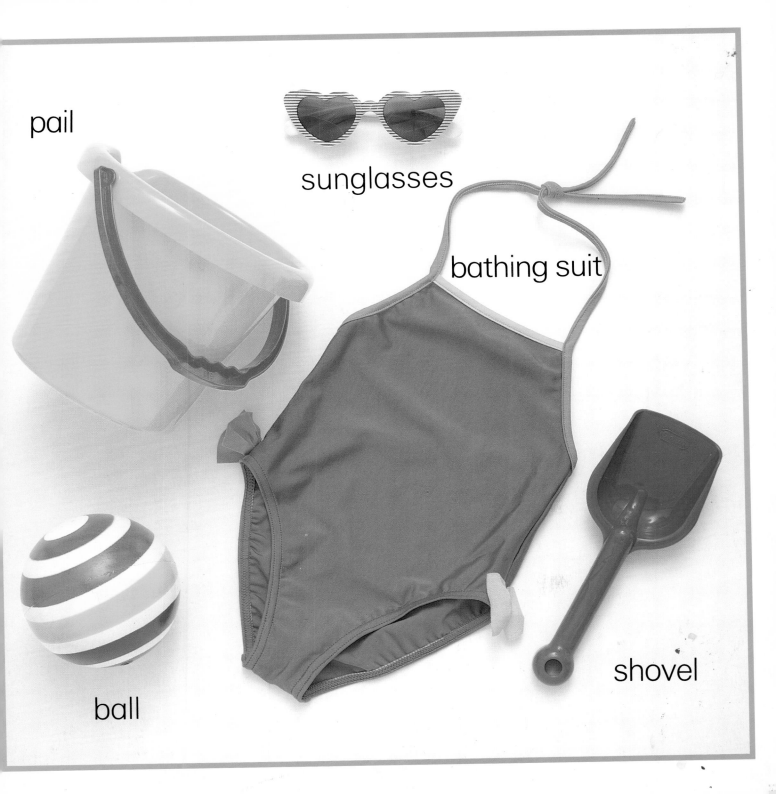

pail

sunglasses

bathing suit

ball

shovel

What's inside
Mommy's
purse?

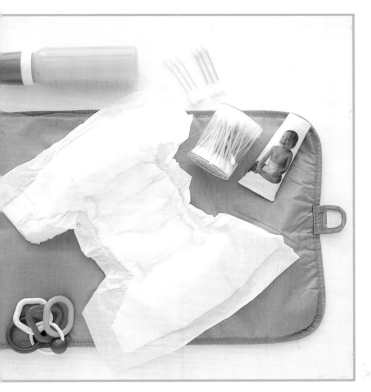

First published in the United States 1990
by Dial Books for Young Readers
A Division of Penguin Books USA Inc.
375 Hudson Street
New York, New York 10014
Published in Great Britain
by Frances Lincoln Ltd
Apollo Works
5 Charlton Kings Road
London NW5 2SB

Concept © 1989 by Frances Lincoln Limited
Photographs © 1989 by Anthea Sieveking
Text © 1989 by Frances Lincoln Limited
All rights reserved
Printed in Hong Kong
E
3 5 7 9 10 8 6 4 2
ISBN 0-8037-0719-3
LC: 89–11897
CIP data available upon request

mirror

comb

keys

change purse

lipstick